Collins

SOLVE IT! BRAIN GAMES FOR BIG THINKERS

Published by Collins
An imprint of HarperCollins Publishers
HarperCollins Publishers
Westerhill Road
Bishopbriggs
Glasgow G64 2QT

www.harpercollins.co.uk

HarperCollins Publishers
1st Floor, Watermarque Building
Ringsend Road
Dublin 4, Ireland

10 9 8 7 6 5 4 3 2

© HarperCollins Publishers 2022
Collins® is a registered trademark of HarperCollins Publishers Limited

All puzzles supplied by Clarity Media Ltd
All images © Shutterstock.com

ISBN 978-0-00-850337-6

Printed and bound in the UK using 100% renewable electricity at CPI Group (UK) Ltd

A catalogue record for this book is available from the British Library.

Publisher: Michelle l'Anson
Project Manager: Sarah Woods
Designer: Kevin Robbins

MIX
Paper from
responsible sources
FSC™ C007454

FSC
www.fsc.org

This book is produced from independently certified
FSC™ paper to ensure responsible forest management.

For more information visit: www.harpercollins.co.uk/green

With more than 120 fun puzzles. you'll
never want to put this book down!

You can do them in any order. but they get harder as
you go through the book so you may wish to start
at the front and work through to the end.

See if you have got them right by checking
out the answers at the back of the book.

There are some blank pages too. which are
handy for jotting down workings. notes.
scribbles or whatever you like!

So... are you ready to

SOLVEIT?

WORDWHEEL

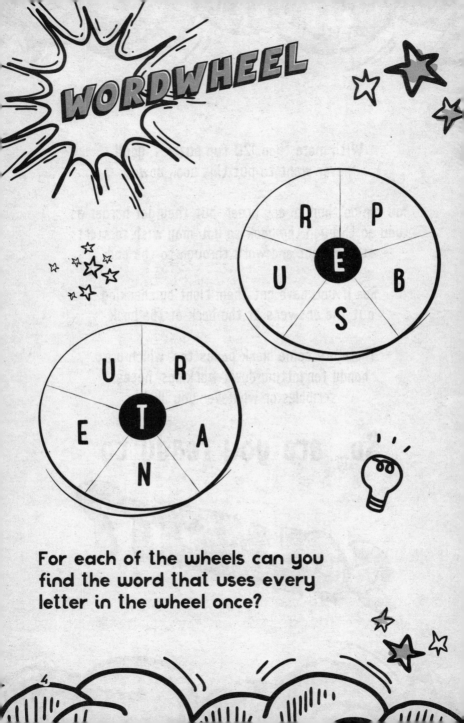

For each of the wheels can you find the word that uses every letter in the wheel once?

4

ANAGRAM CONNECT

Follow the line from each letter at the top and write that letter in the empty circle it is connected to. These letters will spell out the answer word.

MONSTER MATHS

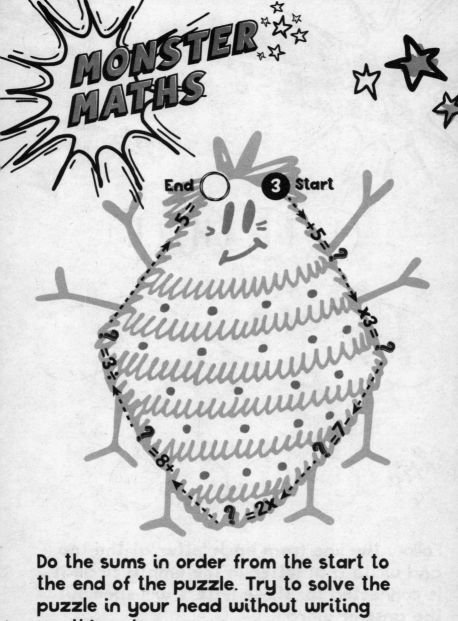

End ○   ③ Start

+5 =?

×3 =?

?=7

?=2x

?=8+

?=3

−5

Do the sums in order from the start to the end of the puzzle. Try to solve the puzzle in your head without writing anything down on paper.

SILHOUETTE

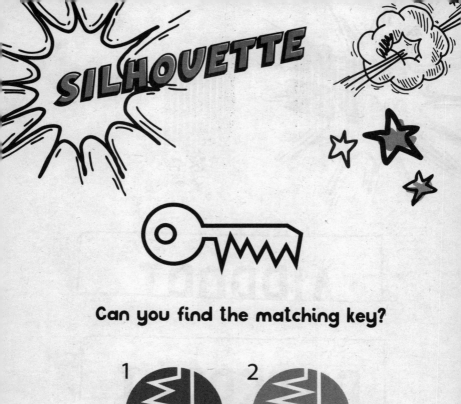

Can you find the matching key?

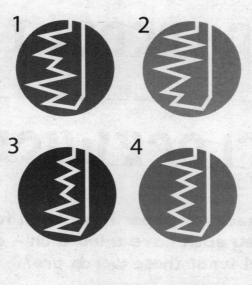

1

2

3

4

FOLDED PAPER

AIRPORT

DIFFERENT

CLOCKWISE

Three pieces of paper have been folded in half. They each have a word on – can you work out what those words are?

BREAK THE CODE

W B D T I L G
A R I E O N P

Can you choose the correct letter from each pair above to reveal a seven-letter word?

(Hint: The first letter of the new word could be W or A.)

FOLLOW THE PATH

B

A

C

Can you work out which kite the hand is holding?

10

MAZE

Find your way through the maze from the entry arrow to the exit arrow.

NUMBER CROSS

Place each of the numbers into the grid. There is only one way to combine them all correctly to fill the grid.

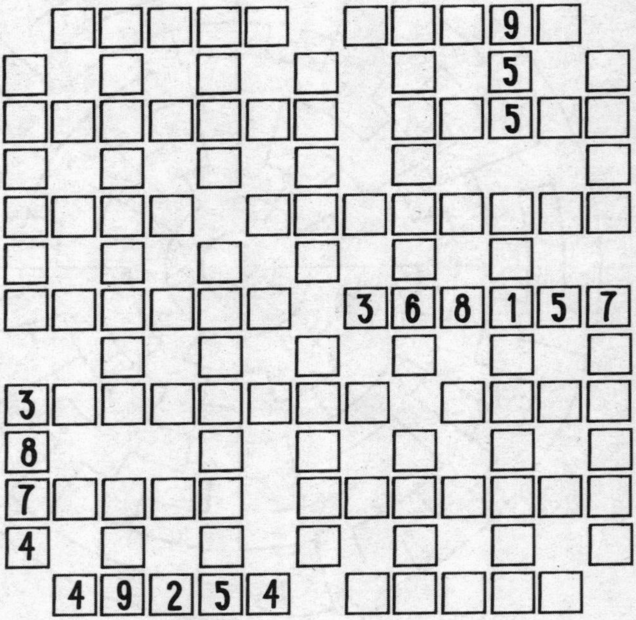

3 numbers
369
~~955~~

4 numbers
1532
~~3874~~
6123
6185
7006
9598

5 numbers
23571
32607
35486
45293
~~49254~~
64269
66805
72300

6 numbers
~~368157~~
371784
732983
792143

7 numbers
3227262
8501824

8 numbers
38021255
52255664
58814095
90658605

9 numbers
442991150
691258880

MISSING VOWELS

SGGSTN

RCTNGL

NDRNTH

YLLW

KNGR

NVTTN

These six words have had their vowels removed. Can you add them back in to find the words?

SUDOKU 4X4

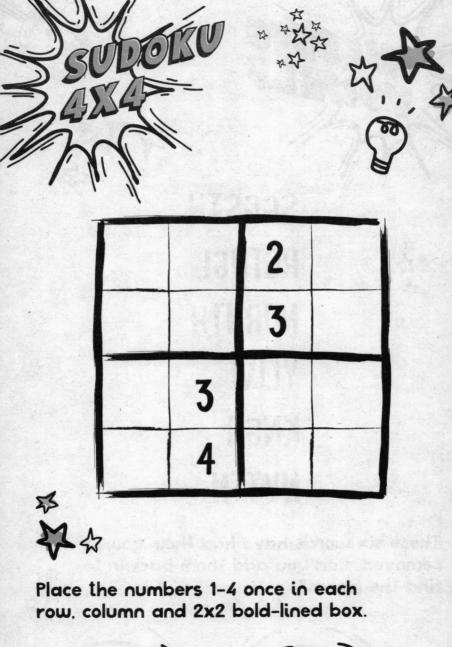

Place the numbers 1-4 once in each
row, column and 2x2 bold-lined box.

NUMBER SQUARE

Enter a number in each of the empty squares to complete the sums correctly. Do the calculations from left-to-right and top-to-bottom rather than in strict mathematical order.

BREAK THE CODE

0	7	3	Two numbers are correct but in the wrong place
9	0	2	One number is correct and in the right place
6	7	0	Two numbers are correct but in the wrong place
4	8	7	One number is correct but in the wrong place
5	3	4	No numbers are correct
			Write the code here

Find the code required to open the safe. The code may use numbers 0-9 only, and no number repeats within the code. Clues alongside each code will help you work out the answer.

PICTURE REVEAL

Colour in the numbers that are part of the 4 times table.

1	41	2	38	25	22	36	40	1	5	1	30	9	46	15
6	13	2	25	45	44	24	28	44	7	31	13	22	46	30
6	20	32	13	42	4	8	1	44	5	3	37	38	7	29
12	16	28	18	22	20	16	36	4	4	45	46	8	8	25
28	20	28	20	5	32	25	24	48	40	22	6	32	12	20
41	36	11	40	22	24	48	40	4	24	41	4	48	29	32
1	4	12	24	40	4	16	16	33	20	9	20	24	36	24
43	23	16	36	8	48	28	32	4	36	20	24	44	44	17
19	10	3	25	26	28	4	46	8	8	44	20	40	9	10
14	26	22	29	46	4	48	32	48	16	41	27	34	43	31
35	7	6	20	4	48	20	28	12	8	12	4	14	29	7
14	33	19	24	31	27	18	31	11	9	10	8	47	15	37
38	41	37	40	36	8	48	44	28	8	20	4	29	6	37
7	37	6	5	12	42	14	37	10	31	36	9	30	41	1
23	11	2	47	48	20	16	16	8	44	16	1	29	1	17

PYRAMID PUZZLE

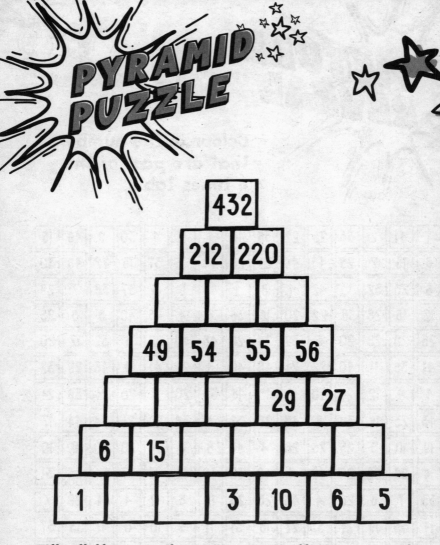

Fill all the empty squares in the pyramid with numbers. Each square contains a number which is the sum of the values in the two squares directly underneath it.

SHAPE MATCH

Can you find three matching shapes in the image that are also identical in size and colour? Shapes may be rotated.

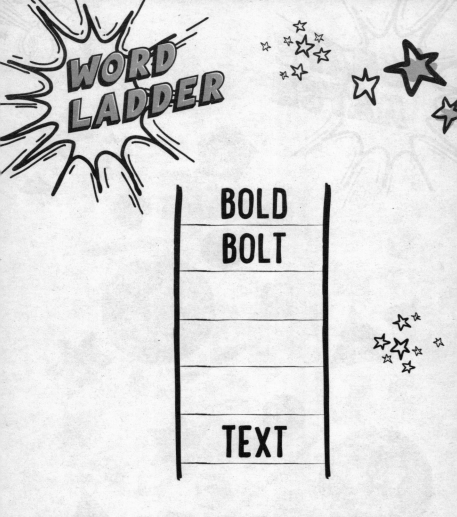

WORD LADDER

BOLD
BOLT
TEXT

Move from the word at the top of the ladder to the word at the bottom of the ladder by changing one letter on each step of the ladder to form a new word. Do not rearrange the order of the letters.

WORD ILLUSION

WET / **DRY**

BUSY / **LAZY**

DUSK / **DAWN**

Pairs of words have been superimposed on top of each other. Can you work out what the words are?

SPOT THE DIFFERENCE

Can you spot the six differences between the two pictures?

MONSTER MATHS

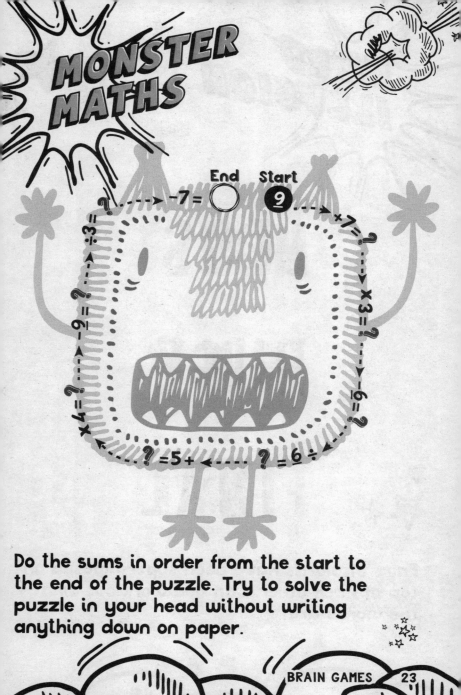

End ◯ **Start** **9**

−7 =

? ÷3

÷6 =

? =

×4 =

? =5+

? = 6 ÷

−6 ?

×3 = ?

? +7

Do the sums in order from the start to the end of the puzzle. Try to solve the puzzle in your head without writing anything down on paper.

WORD ILLUSION

MOSS

HUGE

FINAL

Pairs of words have been superimposed on top of each other. Can you work out what the words are?

NUMBER CROSS

Place each of the numbers into the grid. There is only one way to combine them all correctly to fill the grid.

4 numbers
2588
~~8413~~
8554
9316

5 numbers
16623
32838
42091
60714

6 numbers
128405
171816
260215
759897

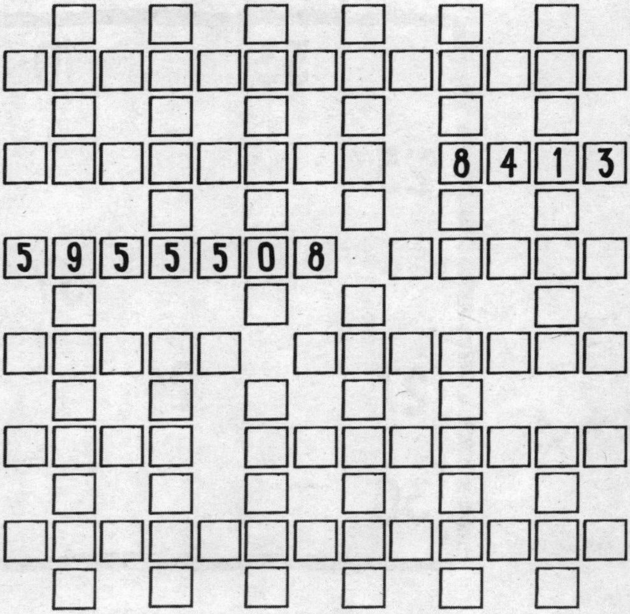

7 numbers
1907741
~~5955508~~
9445305
9969145

8 numbers
28909897
63418274
90055687
94721563

13 numbers
1506845287133
8800096459917

FIND THE SUM

33   10 13

25

37

27   24

30   18

Three of the numbers in the box above add up to 50. But can you work out what those three numbers are?

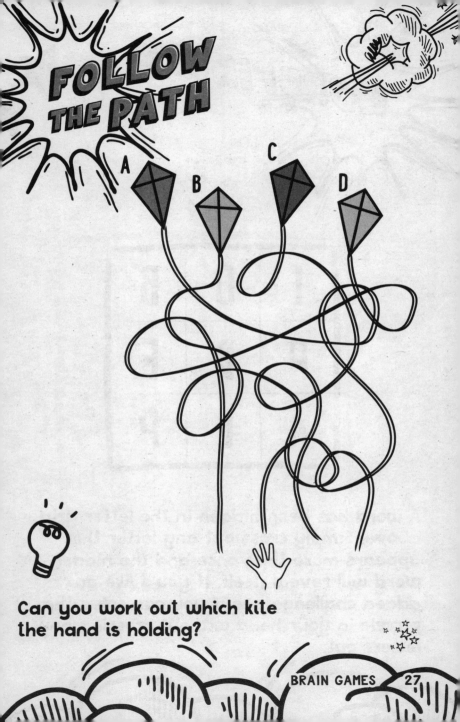

FOLLOW THE PATH

A B C D

Can you work out which kite the hand is holding?

WORDFINDER

I	D	B
P	B	E
A	L	P

A word has been hidden in the letter grid above. Simply cross out any letter that appears more than once and the hidden word will reveal itself. If you'd like an added challenge, see if you can solve the puzzle in your head without crossing any letters out.

SUDOKU 4X4

Place the numbers from 1–4 once in each row, column and 2x2 bold-outlined box.

ANAGRAM CONNECT

Follow the line from each letter at the top and write that letter in the empty circle it is connected to. These letters will spell out the answer word.

MISSING VOWELS

DFFDL

MMMTH

KNWLDG

MSHRM

PSSPRT

THGHTFL

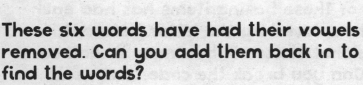

These six words have had their vowels removed. Can you add them back in to find the words?

BREAK THE CODE

GMPVS =

TVHBS =

FHHT =

Each of these baking items has had each letter replaced by the letter before it in the alphabet (so 'B' becomes 'A' and so on). Can you break the code to reveal the answers?

WORDWHEEL

For each of the wheels can you find the word that uses every letter in the wheel once?

NUMBER SQUARE

3	×		+	2	26
+		−		×	
	+		+	9	22
÷		+		×	
	×	5	+		9
10		7		72	

Enter a number in each of the empty squares to complete the sums correctly. Do the calculations from left-to-right and top-to-bottom rather than in strict mathematical order.

PYRAMID PUZZLE

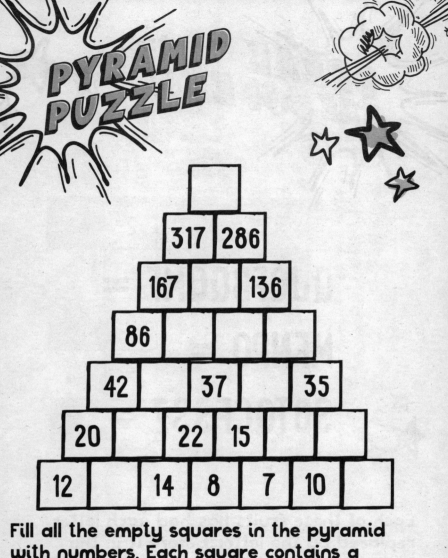

Fill all the empty squares in the pyramid with numbers. Each square contains a number which is the sum of the values in the two squares directly underneath it.

BREAK THE CODE

QJOFBQQMF =

MFNPO =

SBTQCFSSZ =

Each of these fruits has had each letter replaced by the letter before it in the alphabet (so 'B' becomes 'A' and so on). Can you break the code to reveal the answers?

FOLDED PAPER

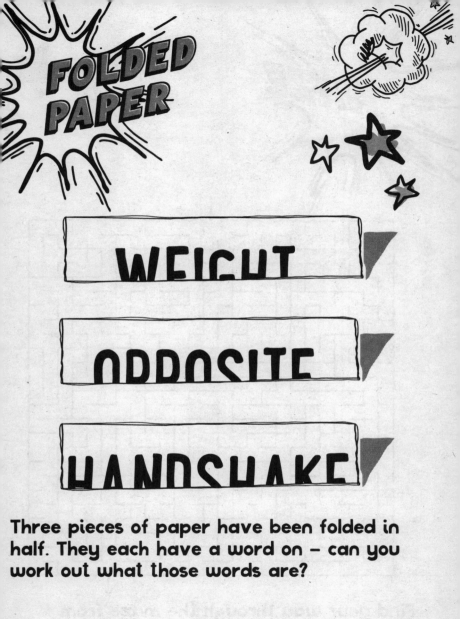

WEIGHT

OPPOSITE

HANDSHAKE

Three pieces of paper have been folded in half. They each have a word on – can you work out what those words are?

MAZE

Find your way through the maze from
the entry arrow to the exit arrow.

SHAPE MATCH

Can you find three matching shapes in the image that are also identical in size and colour? Shapes may be rotated.

SUDOKU 4X4

Place the numbers from 1-4 once in each row, column and 2x2 bold-outlined box.

PILE UP

Can you work out which object is at the bottom of the pile?

SPOT THE DIFFERENCE

Can you spot the six differences between the two pictures?

FIND THE SUM

27		26	30
		37		14
		21	24	22
35			20
		18	17

Three of the numbers in the box above add up to 96. But can you work out what those three numbers are?

MONSTER MATHS

End **Start**
4

÷4=

×6=
?

+11=?

+3=
?

?÷2=

?=3×

?=7

Do the sums in order from the start to the end of the puzzle. Try to solve the puzzle in your head without writing anything down on paper.

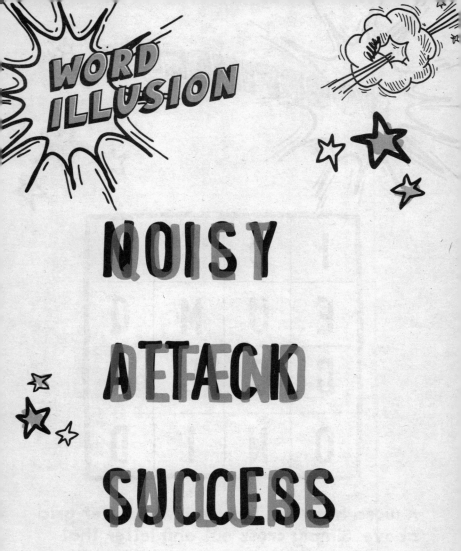

NOISY

ATTACK

SUCCESS

Pairs of words have been superimposed on top of each other. Can you work out what the words are?

WORDFINDER

I	U	X	L
E	U	M	Q
D	Q	D	X
O	N	I	D

A word has been hidden in the letter grid above. Simply cross out any letter that appears more than once and the hidden word will reveal itself. If you'd like an added challenge, see if you can solve the puzzle in your head without crossing any letters out.

CROSSWORD

Across

4 Not awake (6)
6 Birds of prey that hoot (4)
7 Flower given on Valentine's Day (4)
8 Metallic element (4)
9 Item used to catch fish (3)
10 What a beach is made of (4)
11 Alternative to a bath (6)

Down

1 Person who goes into space (9)
2 Saturdays and Sundays collectively (8)
3 Trick-or-treating happens on this day (9)
5 Place (8)

KRISS KROSS

Place all the words into the grid once each to complete the puzzle.

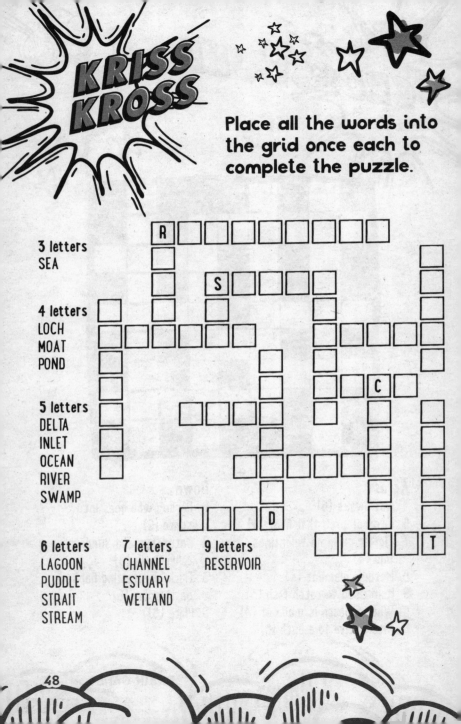

3 letters
SEA

4 letters
LOCH
MOAT
POND

5 letters
DELTA
INLET
OCEAN
RIVER
SWAMP

6 letters
LAGOON
PUDDLE
STRAIT
STREAM

7 letters
CHANNEL
ESTUARY
WETLAND

9 letters
RESERVOIR

WORD LADDER

WILD

WELD

BEES

Move from the word at the top of the ladder to the word at the bottom of the ladder by changing one letter on each step of the ladder to form a new word. Do not rearrange the order of the letters.

FOLLOW THE PATH

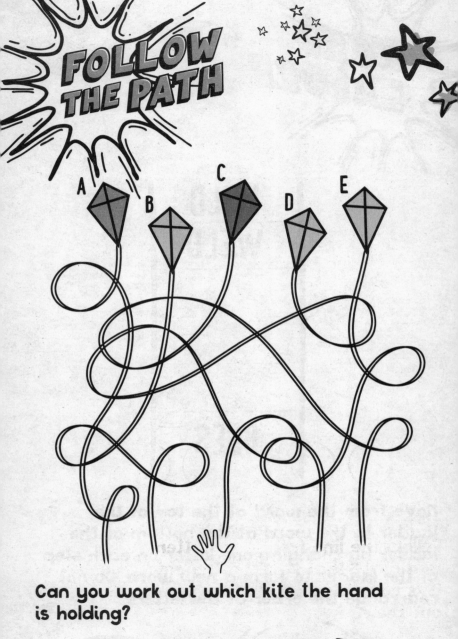

Can you work out which kite the hand is holding?

ANAGRAM CONNECT

Follow the line from each letter at the top and write that letter in the empty circle it is connected to. These letters will spell out the answer word.

SILHOUETTE

Can you find the matching key?

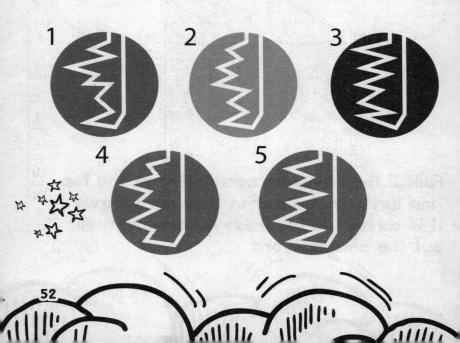

PICTURE REVEAL

Colour in the numbers that are part of the 7 times table.

32	39	45	62	65	4	7	49	49	63	84	70	56	28	83
51	22	45	18	14	49	77	14	42	56	35	16	49	70	12
80	24	28	63	84	49	28	7	28	84	52	84	9	42	53
48	49	14	56	35	70	56	7	711	80	7	42	21	7	9
28	56	84	35	28	70	9	17	40	43	37	49	64	63	30
84	70	28	35	78	45	9	1	7	51	29	13	82	70	18
42	63	77	5	51	52	2	48	16	31	80	37	47	14	70
63	63	50	26	63	34	83	77	71	55	13	77	18	53	7
57	56	21	83	40	34	49	35	21	51	57	8	66	12	49
11	80	14	63	49	20	43	28	68	79	53	42	66	18	70
60	11	20	42	63	14	82	47	53	27	84	14	56	19	14
83	8	83	11	84	28	77	84	74	19	37	28	27	59	14
50	26	68	65	27	77	77	70	70	81	45	81	34	31	70
72	81	34	50	61	51	48	35	77	70	84	63	1	84	28
41	16	78	4	68	73	51	10	17	54	21	21	28	49	65

PYRAMID PUZZLE

Fill all the empty squares in the pyramid
with numbers. Each square contains
a number which is the sum of the values
in the two squares directly underneath it.

BREAK THE CODE

1	2	5	One number is correct but in the wrong place
1	9	2	One number is correct but in the wrong place
5	9	0	No numbers are correct
2	8	7	Two numbers are correct but in the wrong place
5	0	1	One number is correct and in the right place
			Write the code here

Find the code required to open the safe. The code may use numbers 0–9 only, and no number repeats within the code. Clues alongside each code will help you work out the answer.

WORDSEARCH

Find each of the words in the grid. Words may be hidden horizontally or vertically.

```
S  E  S  H  A  R  M  O  N  I  C  A
A  T  R  O  M  B  O  N  E  T  Y  G
X  P  F  P  B  C  L  Q  C  R  A  T
O  E  L  H  U  L  T  T  E  U  R  K
P  M  U  A  I  A  U  O  L  M  U  O
H  V  T  R  W  R  B  B  L  P  K  L
O  W  E  P  O  I  A  O  O  E  U  W
N  R  P  I  A  N  O  E  R  T  L  S
E  S  I  Y  R  E  C  O  R  D  E  R
V  I  O  L  A  T  N  W  S  R  L  M
H  Y  T  I  S  T  S  E  O  I  E  R
E  O  L  R  Y  G  U  I  T  A  R  T
```

CELLO	HARP	TROMBONE
CLARINET	OBOE	TRUMPET
FLUTE	PIANO	TUBA
GUITAR	RECORDER	UKULELE
HARMONICA	SAXOPHONE	VIOLA

SUDOKU 4X4

Place the numbers from 1-4 once in each
row, column and 2x2 bold-outlined box.

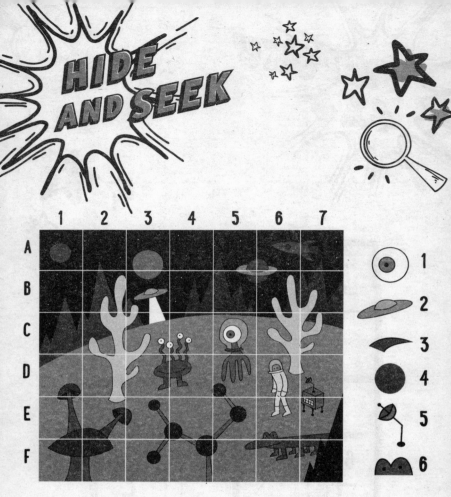

HIDE AND SEEK

Find the squares, from A1 to F7, that contain the numbered objects shown at the right-hand edge of the grid. These objects may have been increased in size, but their colour and shape remain the same, and they are never rotated or mirrored.

SUDOKU 6X6

Place the numbers from 1-6 once in each row, column and 3x2 bold-outlined box.

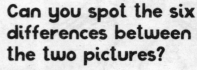

SPOT THE DIFFERENCE

Can you spot the six differences between the two pictures?

KRISS KROSS

Place all the words into the grid once each to complete the puzzle.

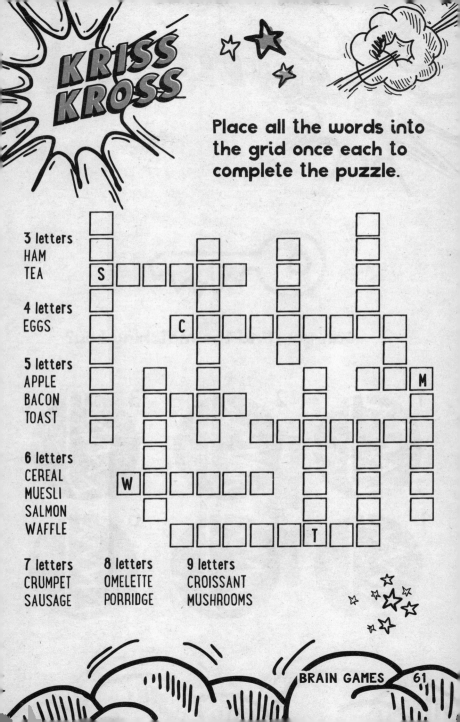

3 letters
HAM
TEA

4 letters
EGGS

5 letters
APPLE
BACON
TOAST

6 letters
CEREAL
MUESLI
SALMON
WAFFLE

7 letters
CRUMPET
SAUSAGE

8 letters
OMELETTE
PORRIDGE

9 letters
CROISSANT
MUSHROOMS

SILHOUETTE

Can you find the matching key?

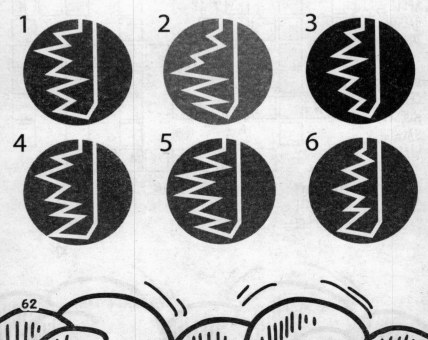

1

2

3

4

5

6

MONSTER MATHS

End ÷5= 7 Start ×4

+9= ? ? +5= ?

?=3÷ ?=3x

?=2x

Do the sums in order from the start to the end of the puzzle. Try to solve the puzzle in your head without writing anything down on paper.

PICTURE REVEAL

Colour in the numbers that are part of the 8 times table.

96	8	24	88	16	59	25	15	78	43	52	46	15	3	77
40	54	69	55	32	64	71	14	66	45	3	63	29	95	39
32	44	29	62	34	40	39	49	35	35	62	67	62	89	63
8	80	90	92	27	24	80	59	64	8	96	40	47	6	59
42	64	6	21	77	31	8	72	96	59	3	56	8	40	86
50	48	85	4	85	2	56	54	67	2	54	42	15	64	28
61	16	8	60	30	56	88	94	73	62	64	32	72	96	1
22	59	24	8	48	56	32	40	64	32	88	10	82	1	65
80	96	57	25	18	96	16	80	88	40	14	77	87	43	13
72	37	1	91	40	16	96	64	64	40	72	69	63	94	47
16	85	92	6	32	24	76	96	8	96	80	40	84	41	31
16	90	70	34	24	88	72	36	72	64	80	24	72	74	55
88	51	80	64	16	96	80	48	59	72	96	88	72	88	32
32	11	72	79	79	59	40	40	32	45	48	64	40	72	64
40	8	48	59	71	36	82	28	16	80	64	24	8	96	73

MAZE

Find your way through the maze from the entry arrow to the exit arrow.

WORDWHEEL

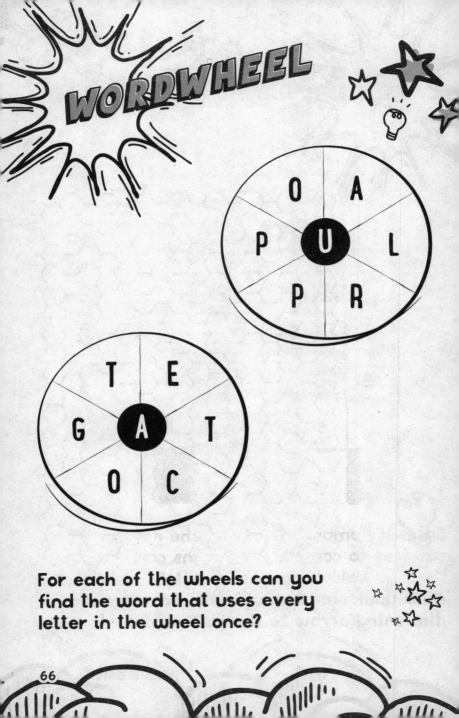

For each of the wheels can you find the word that uses every letter in the wheel once?

NUMBER SQUARE

Enter a number in each of the empty squares to complete the sums correctly. Perform calculations from left-to-right and top-to-bottom rather than in strict mathematical order.

SUDOKU 6X6

Place the numbers from 1–6 once in each row, column and 3x2 bold-outlined box.

WORDSEARCH

Find each of the words in the grid. Words may be hidden horizontally, vertically or diagonally.

```
W G E T N H P E E L E R
R O A R S B A D G X A T
O K O R S A E W R U T I
L N F D L K U W A U O M
L I R W E I L C T Z N E
I V Y H E N C X E U G R
N E I I O G S P R P S A
G S N S T R P R T A A A
P F G K H R Z S O E H N
I O P P L A T E S O S O
N R A L X Y U N C E N S
T K N S P A T U L A F W
```

BAKING TRAY   KNIVES   SPATULA

FORK   PEELER   TIMER

FRYING PAN   PLATES   TONGS

GARLIC PRESS   ROLLING PIN   WHISK

GRATER   SAUCEPAN   WOODEN SPOON

BREAK THE CODE

XBTQ =

CFFUMF =

CVUUFSGMZ =

Each of these insects has had each letter replaced by the letter before it in the alphabet (so 'B' becomes 'A' and so on). Can you break the code to reveal the answers?

PILE UP

Can you work out which object is at the bottom of the pile?

FOLLOW THE PATH

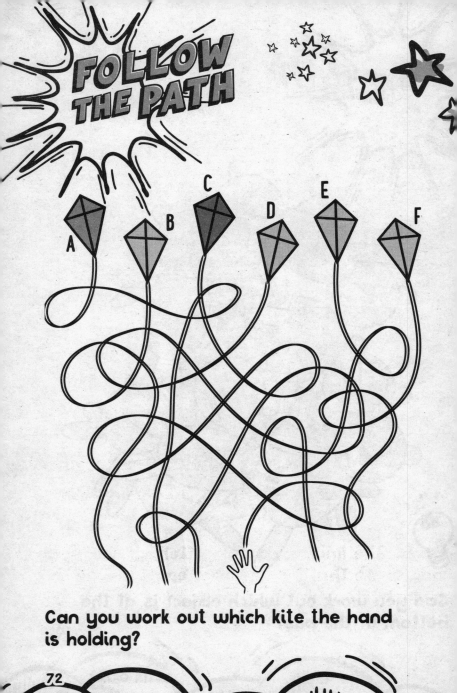

Can you work out which kite the hand is holding?

ANAGRAM CONNECT

Follow the line from each letter at the top and write that letter in the empty circle it is connected to. These letters will spell out the answer word.

ANAGRAMS

HUG LATER

FRY COAT

DAY BROKE

GREET CLAN

MINT GAMES

IN QUOTES

Can you rearrange the scrambled letters to reveal six new words?

NUMBER CROSS

Place each of the numbers into the grid. There is only one way to combine them all correctly to fill the grid.

4 numbers
1034
1715
3986
4184
~~4547~~
6167

5 numbers
33225
47444
47489
98306

6 numbers
344329
393020
410452
704797

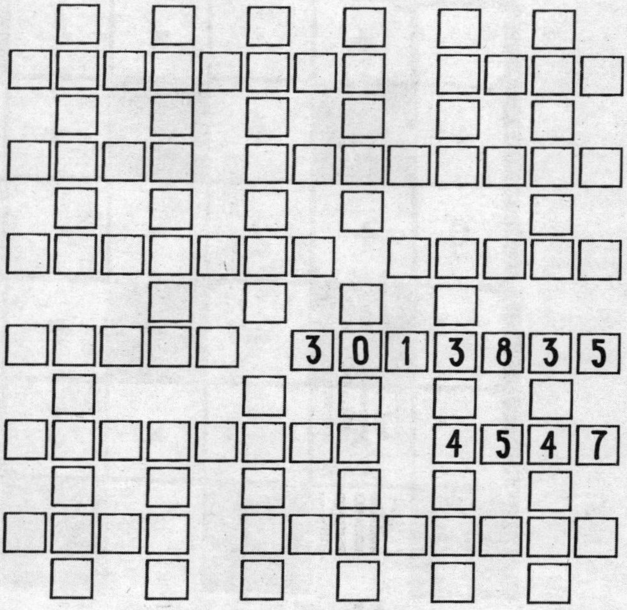

7 numbers
2034086
~~3013835~~
8042043
9255042

8 numbers
37384602
47850327
59004549
79299268
79344248
84765784

NUMBER SQUARE

Enter a number in each of the empty squares to complete the sums correctly. Do the calculations from left-to-right and top-to-bottom rather than in strict mathematical order.

HIDE AND SEEK

Find the squares, from A1 to F7, that contain the numbered objects shown at the right-hand edge of the grid. These objects may have been increased in size, but their colour and shape remain the same, and they are never rotated or mirrored.

KAKURO

If you haven't tried a kakuro puzzle before here is an example to give you a helping hand.

Follow the instructions below, using the solution diagram to help guide you.

Kakuro sample

Kakuro sample solution

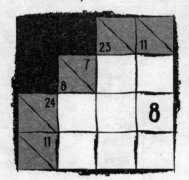

For a total 8. you could have 1 and 7. 2 and 6 or 3 and 5 but not 4 and 4.

Use numbers 1–9 to fill in the empty squares.

- **The total of each horizontal block of cells equals the clue number on its left.**
- **The total of each vertical block of cells equals the clue number at the top.**
- **Each number can be used only once in each block.**

KAKURO

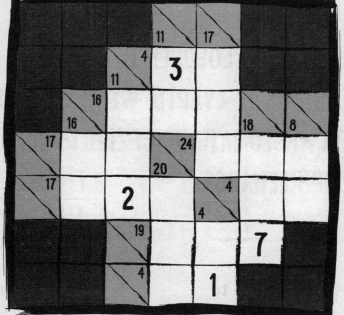

Now try this kakuro puzzle yourself.

BREAK THE CODE

TWHHIQSD CLOEDPEK UZSVEWSV
EEXGTCRKAZ LVEPTDTWEGRTSY TVOR
MQAWKGEO IATC DCIJFZFLILCGUBLUTA
TZOP REEHADDF

Can you work out how to extract a
meaningful sentence from the seemingly
random series of letters above?

PYRAMID PUZZLE

Fill all the empty squares in the pyramid with numbers. Each square contains a number which is the sum of the values in the two squares directly underneath it.

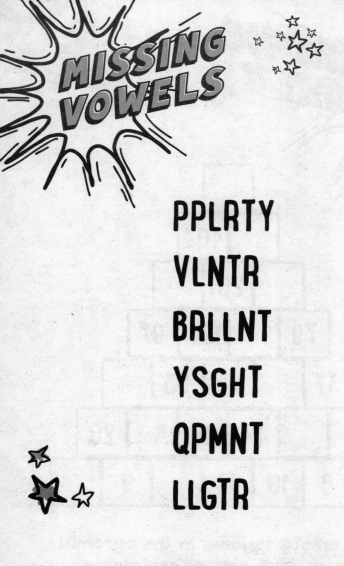

MISSING VOWELS

PPLRTY

VLNTR

BRLLNT

YSGHT

QPMNT

LLGTR

These six words have had their vowels removed. Can you add them back in to find the words?

SPOT THE DIFFERENCE

Can you spot the six differences between the two pictures?

CROSSWORD

Across
4 Animal that feeds on other animals (9)
6 Consumed food (3)
8 Extremely precise (5)
9 Opposite of loose (5)
10 A long period of time (3)
12 Speech sound that is not a vowel (9)

Down
1 The opposite of future (4)
2 One _____ : boy band (9)
3 Move around in a circle (6)
5 Additional (5)
6 Room inside the roof of a house (5)
7 Part of a car (6)
11 Object worn on a finger (4)

WORD LADDER

NICE

PETS

Move from the word at the top of the ladder to the word at the bottom of the ladder by changing one letter on each step of the ladder to form a new word. Do not rearrange the order of the letters.

(Note that there may be more than one way to solve the puzzle. Word ladders often have multiple solutions.)

FIND THE SUM

```
              14    22   32
        30    43
        29    28
   25   15               35
                    12   23
```

Three of the numbers in the box above add up to 102. But can you work out what those three numbers are?

SHAPE MATCH

Can you find three matching shapes in the image that are also identical in size and colour? Shapes may be rotated.

KRISS KROSS

Place all the words into the grid once each to complete the puzzle.

4 letters
THAI

5 letters
CZECH
DUTCH
GREEK
HINDI

6 letters
ARABIC
FRENCH
GERMAN
POLISH

7 letters
ITALIAN
PERSIAN
RUSSIAN
SWEDISH
TURKISH

8 letters
JAPANESE
MANDARIN

SUDOKU 6X6

Place the numbers from 1–6 once in each row, column and 3x2 bold-outlined box.

BREAK THE CODE

8	1	0	One number is correct but in the wrong place
0	1	4	No numbers are correct
3	1	0	One number is correct and in the right place
7	1	6	One number is correct but in the wrong place
5	6	1	One number is correct and in the right place
			Write the code here

Find the code required to open the safe. The code may use numbers 0–9 only, and no number repeats within the code. Clues alongside each code will help you work out the answer.

ANAGRAMS

CAN ENTER

MAY DRIP

YOUNG HERD

TRUE NOVEL

LIVE BEE

PART FIGURE

Can you rearrange the scrambled letters
to reveal six new words?

SILHOUETTE

Can you find the matching key?

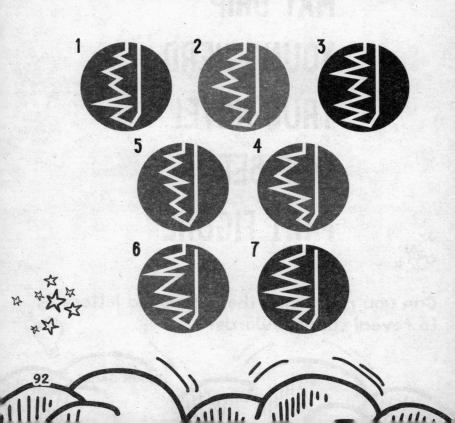

KAKURO

See page 78 for help to complete this puzzle

Use numbers 1–9 to fill in the empty squares.
- The total of each horizontal block of cells equals the clue number on its left.
- The total of each vertical block of cells equals the clue number at the top.
- Each number can be used only once in each block.

HIDE AND SEEK

Find the squares, from A1 to F7, that contain the numbered objects shown at the right-hand edge of the grid. These objects may have been increased in size, but their colour and shape remain the same, and they are never rotated or mirrored.

WORD SPLITS

EAPPLE PIN

DER THUN

SION DECI

These three words have been split into smaller sections and shuffled around. Can you put them back in order?

NUMBER SQUARE

6	+		+		**23**
÷		×		÷	
	×		+	1	**7**
×		+		×	
5	×		×	7	**140**
10		**22**		**56**	

Enter a number in each of the empty squares to complete the sums correctly. Do the calculations from left-to-right and top-to-bottom rather than in strict mathematical order.

96

PICTURE REVEAL

Colour in the numbers that are part of the 9 times table.

20	31	60	45	108	72	27	36	27	90	99	9	32	41	47
34	1	18	90	95	30	2	59	40	66	73	81	90	67	97
33	54	9	41	47	2	32	38	87	23	85	56	108	99	57
36	45	55	44	17	89	65	107	40	103	101	51	7	18	36
90	36	76	28	27	99	34	88	69	9	81	95	70	30	18
81	96	56	21	45	40	51	66	52	72	1	69	8	25	36
36	86	20	19	45	90	80	62	19	27	63	103	53	31	36
54	70	76	78	5	13	79	38	35	91	50	102	74	79	45
90	85	81	36	96	25	67	91	50	58	59	45	90	50	108
36	17	64	36	94	60	104	66	53	84	56	36	46	43	81
72	68	7	81	99	81	71	95	2	18	9	81	23	86	9
9	90	16	25	33	90	99	90	36	108	50	79	20	54	108
50	45	90	65	15	5	51	105	4	28	75	43	63	18	107
12	83	54	72	25	26	80	102	103	73	94	9	72	46	56
32	40	8	81	72	108	54	27	27	36	108	54	52	66	35

**Find your way through the maze from
the entry arrow to the exit arrow.**

BREAK THE CODE

XBWF =

QFCCMFT =

MJGFHVBSE =

Each of these beach items has had each
letter replaced by the letter before it in
the alphabet (so 'B' becomes 'A' and so
on). Can you break the code to reveal
the answers?

WORD LADDER

MILD

RAIN

Move from the word at the top of the ladder to the word at the bottom of the ladder by changing one letter on each step of the ladder to form a new word. Do not rearrange the order of the letters.

(Note that there may be more than one way to solve the puzzle. Word ladders often have multiple solutions.)

MISSING VOWELS

VLNCH

TGRPH

SHPHRD

WDNSDY

NSTNT

PCFL

These six words have had their vowels removed. Can you add them back in to find the words?

NUMBER CROSS

Place each of the numbers into the grid. There is only one way to combine them all correctly to fill the grid.

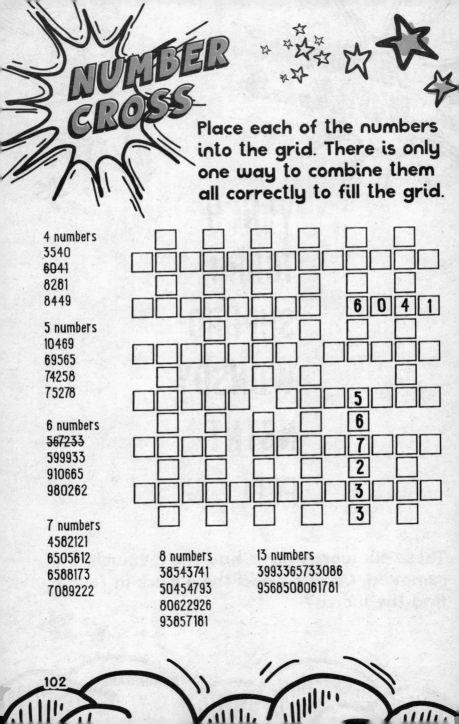

4 numbers
3540
6041 ~~6041~~
8281
8449

5 numbers
10469
69565
74258
75278

6 numbers
567233 ~~567233~~
599933
910665
980262

7 numbers
4582121
6505612
6588173
7089222

8 numbers
38543741
50454793
80622926
93857181

13 numbers
3993365733086
9568508061781

NUMBER SQUARE

	+	3	÷	1	**10**
+		×		×	
	÷		+		**11**
÷		+		×	
5	×	2	−		**4**
3		**14**		**54**	

Enter a number in each of the empty
squares to complete the sums correctly.
Do the calculations from left-to-right
and top-to-bottom rather than in strict
mathematical order.

SUDOKU 6X6

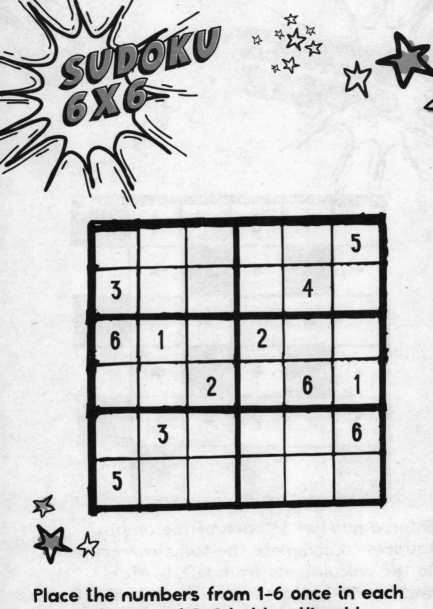

Place the numbers from 1-6 once in each
row, column and 3x2 bold-outlined box.

HIDE AND SEEK

Find the squares, from A1 to F7, that contain the numbered objects shown at the right-hand edge of the grid. These objects may have been increased in size, but their colour and shape remain the same, and they are never rotated or mirrored.

WORDSEARCH

Find each of the words in the grid. Words may be hidden horizontally, vertically or diagonally and either a forwards or backwards direction.

```
Z G N I R A E B S A E R
O X S R A E G H E P A H
R F M R E B Z B H V A T
T R B O R T U C X N L E
E A E L J T K A D R A L
K M L U R B V L C C D E
S E L E R U E F H A E Y
A I N A R B V X A B P E
B N K C A O Z R I L J K
I E N R M K K O N E J T
I W S B L E E H W I J F
K R O F S P O K E S X K
```

BASKET   BRAKE   EYELET   GEARS   PEDAL

BEARING   CABLE   FORK   HANDLEBARS   SPOKES

BELL   CHAIN   FRAME   INNER TUBE   WHEEL

CROSSWORD

Across
4 Observe: see (6)
6 Opposite of early (4)
7 Eon (anag.) (3)
8 Parts of the mouth (4)
9 Part of an apple containing the pips (4)
10 Take part in a play (3)
11 List of food items at a restaurant (4)
12 Dried grape (6)

Down
1 E.g. Asia or Europe (9)
2 Creature such as triceratops (8)
3 Amuse (9)
5 ____ eel: type of fish (8)

SHAPE MATCH

Can you find three matching shapes in the image that are also identical in size and colour? Shapes may be rotated.

WORD SPLITS

AMB   NCE   ULA

EMER   CY   GEN

ICU   DIFF   LT

These three words have been split into smaller sections and shuffled around. Can you put them back in order?

KAKURO

See page 78 for help to complete this puzzle

Use numbers 1–9 to fill in the empty squares.

- The total of each horizontal block of cells equals the clue number on its left.
- The total of each vertical block of cells equals the clue number at the top.
- Each number can be used only once in each block.

WORDWHEEL

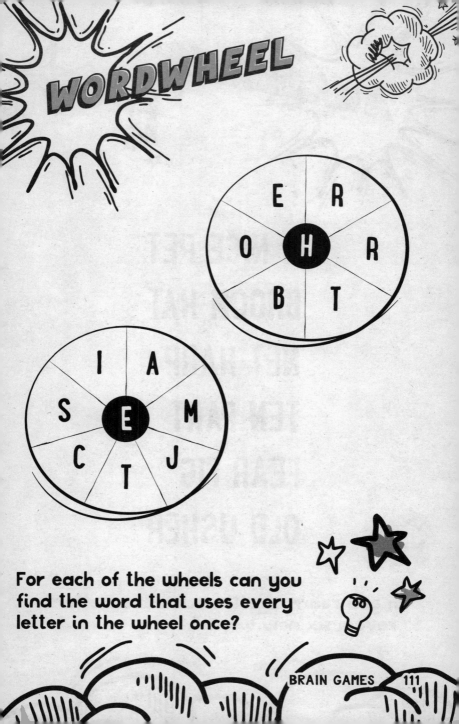

For each of the wheels can you find the word that uses every letter in the wheel once?

ANAGRAMS

A NICE PET

BROOM HAT

NET HARP

TEN PART

FEAR FIG

OLD USHER

Can you rearrange the scrambled letters
to reveal six new words?

BREAK THE CODE

8	1	0	One number is correct but in the wrong place
0	1	4	No numbers are correct
3	1	0	One number is correct and in the right place
7	1	6	One number is correct but in the wrong place
5	6	1	One number is correct and in the right place
			Write the code here

Find the code required to open the safe. The code may use numbers 0–9 only, and no number repeats within the code. Clues alongside each code will help you work out the answer.

FIND THE SUM

			38
28		30	22
	36	18	
39		32	
14	24	40	35

Three of the numbers in the box above add up to 112. But can you work out what those three numbers are?

WORD ILLUSION

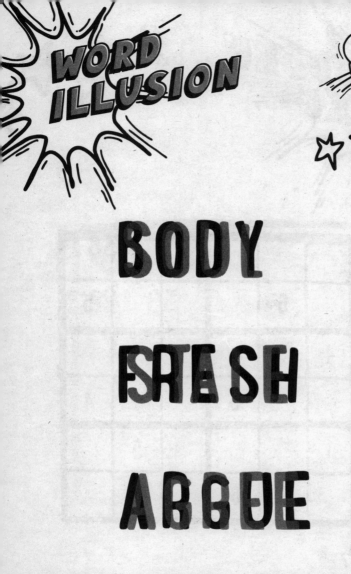

BODY

FRESH

ARGUE

Pairs of words have been superimposed on top of each other. Can you work out what the words are?

SUDOKU 6X6

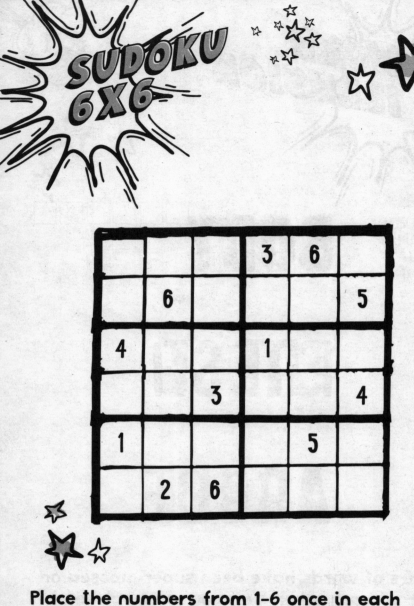

Place the numbers from 1-6 once in each row, column and 3x2 bold-outlined box.

KRISS KROSS

Place all the words into the grid once each to complete the puzzle.

3 letters
HUM
TAP
ZAP

4 letters
BANG
BEEP
FIZZ
HONK
PLOP
TOOT

5 letters
CHOMP
COUGH
KNOCK
SPLAT
THUMP

6 letters
HICCUP
SIZZLE
SPLASH
WHOOSH

7 letters
CRACKLE

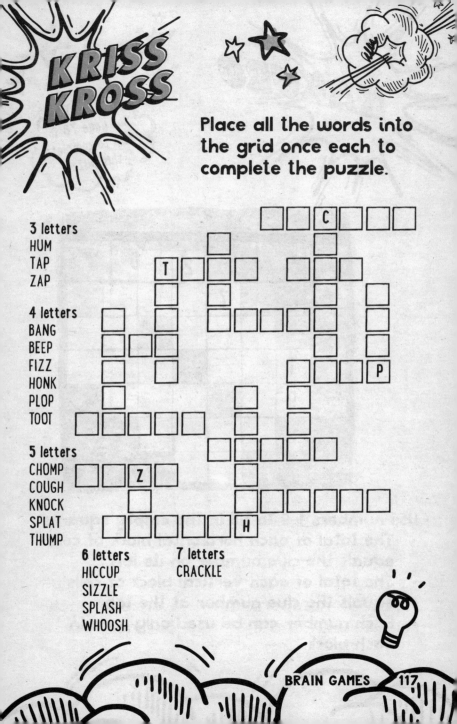

KAKURO

See page 78 for help to complete this puzzle

Use numbers 1-9 to fill in the empty squares.

- The total of each horizontal block of cells equals the clue number on its left.
- The total of each vertical block of cells equals the clue number at the top.
- Each number can be used only once in each block.

CROSSWORD

Across
1 Opportunity (6)
6 This follows morning (9)
7 A sweet fruit (4)
8 Find pleasant (4)
9 A surgical procedure (9)
11 Road (6)

Down
1 Winner (8)
2 A mammal with a long snout and sticky tongue (8)
3 Vehicle (3)
4 Opposite of negative (8)
5 Global computer network you use to visit websites (8)
10 Creative school subject (3)

ER EV SR EE CA PH IA OR LF TE ET
SR OT ER DA HT SI

**Can you work out what you must do
to each pair of letters above in order
to crack the code and spell out the
answer message?**

ANAGRAMS

FACE PERIL

DO WASH

LEAN GRIN

THIRD BAY

NATURE STAR

NEXT EMPIRE

Can you rearrange the scrambled letters
to reveal six new words?

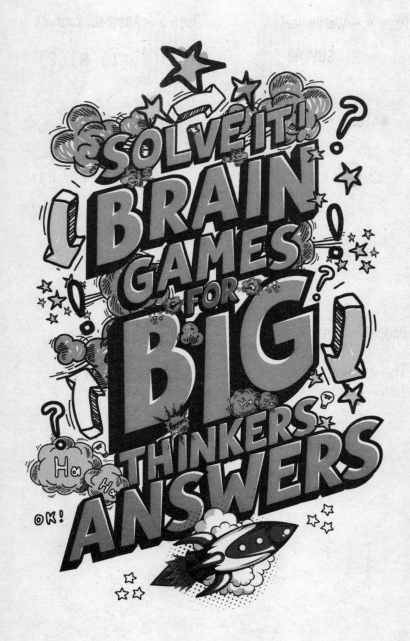

Page 4 – Wordwheel

SUPERB

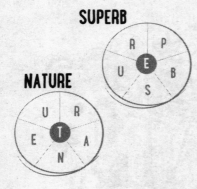

NATURE

Page 5 – Anagram connect

Page 6 – Monster maths

The answer is 9

Page 7 – Silhouette

The answer is 4

Page 8 – Folded paper

AIRPORT
DIFFERENT
CLOCKWISE

Page 9 – Break the code

WRITING

Page 10 – Follow the path

The answer is A

Page 11 – Maze

Page 12 - Number crosss

```
6 4 2 6 9     4 5 2 9 3
7   4   1   3   2   5   6
3 2 2 7 2 6 2   2 3 5 7 1
2   9   3   6   5       8
9 5 9 8   9 0 6 5 8 6 0 5
8   1   5   7   6   9
3 7 1 7 8 4   3 6 8 1 5 7
    5   8   3   4   2   9
3 8 0 2 1 2 5 5   1 5 3 2
8       4   4   7   8   1
7 2 3 0 0   8 5 0 1 8 2 4
4   6   9   6   0   8   3
    4 9 2 5 4   6 6 8 0 5
```

Page 13 - Missing vowels

SUGGESTION

RECTANGLE

UNDERNEATH

YELLOW

KANGAROO

INVITATION

Page 14 - Sudoku 4x4

3	1	2	4
4	2	3	1
1	3	4	2
2	4	1	3

Page 15 - Number square

4	x	2	x	1	8
+		+		+	
8	+	9	+	6	23
x		-		x	
5	x	3	+	7	22
60		8		49	

Page 16 – Break the code
The answer is 701

Page 17 – Picture reveal
CACTUS

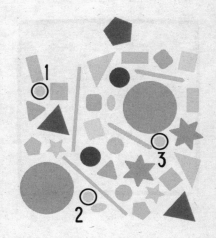

Page 18 – Pyramid puzzle

			432			
		212	220			
	103	109	111			
	49	54	55	56		
21	28	26	29	27		
6	15	13	13	16	11	
1	5	10	3	10	6	5

Page 19 – Shape match

Page 20 – Word ladder

BOLD
BOLT
BELT
BEST
TEST
TEXT

Page 21 – Word illusion

WET   DRY

BUSY   LAZY

DUSK   DAWN

Page 22 – Spot the difference

Page 23 – Monster maths

The answer is 6

Page 24 – Word illusion

LESS MORE

HUGE TINY

FINAL FIRST

Page 25 – Number cross

```
8   2   9   3   1   6
1 5 0 6 8 4 5 2 8 7 1 3 3
  5   0   4   8   1   4
9 4 7 2 1 5 6 3   8 4 1 3
    1   3   8   1   8
5 9 5 5 5 0 8   1 6 6 2 3
    0     5   9       7
6 0 7 1 4   1 9 0 7 7 4 1
  5   2   4   6   5
2 5 8 8   2 8 9 0 9 8 9 7
  6   4   0   1   8   3
8 8 0 0 0 9 6 4 5 9 9 1 7
  7   5   1   5   7   6
```

Page 26 – Find the sum

The answer is
10. 13. 27

Page 27 – Follow the path

The answer is B

Page 28 – Wordfinder

IDEAL

Page 29 – Sudoku 4x4

1	4	2	3
2	3	4	1
4	1	3	2
3	2	1	4

Page 30 – Anagram connect

C A R E S

R A C E S

Page 31 – Missing vowels

DAFFODIL
MAMMOTH
KNOWLEDGE
MUSHROOM
PASSPORT
THOUGHTFUL

Page 32 – Break the code

FLOUR
SUGAR
EGGS

Page 33 – Wordwheel

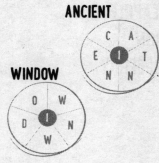

ANCIENT

C A
E I T
N N

WINDOW

O W
D I N
W

Page 34 – Number square

3	x	8	+	2	26
+	■	-	■	x	
7	+	6	+	9	22
÷	■	+	■	x	
1	x	5	+	4	9
10		7		72	

Page 35 – Pyramid puzzle

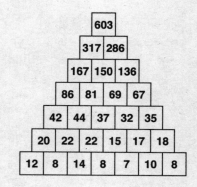

```
            603
        317   286
      167  150  136
     86  81  69  67
   42  44  37  32  35
  20  22  22  15  17  18
12  8  14  8  7  10  8
```

Page 36 – Break the code

PINEAPPLE
LEMON
RASPBERRY

Page 37 – Folded paper

WEIGHT
OPPOSITE
HANDSHAKE

Page 38 – Maze

Page 39 – Shape match

Page 40 – Sudoku 4x4

1	3	4	2
2	4	3	1
3	2	1	4
4	1	2	3

Page 41 – Pile up

Page 42 – Spot the difference

Page 43 – Find the sum

The answer is
24. 35. 37

Page 44 – Monster maths

The answer is 13

Page 45 – Word illusion

NOISY   QUIET

ATTACK   DEFEND

SUCCESS   FAILURE

Page 46 – Wordfinder

LEMON

Page 47 – Crossword

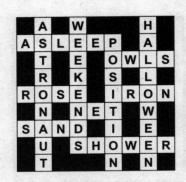

Page 48 – Kriss kross

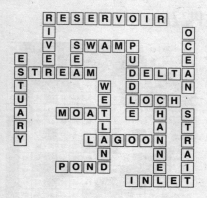

Page 49 – Word ladder

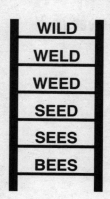

WILD
WELD
WEED
SEED
SEES
BEES

Page 50 – Follow the path

The answer is D

Page 51 – Anagram connect

Page 52 – Silhouette

The answer is 2

Page 53 – Picture reveal

PIZZA

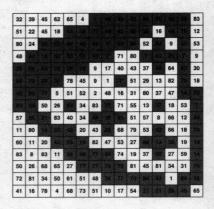

Page 54 – Pyramid puzzle

```
                  758
              395     363
          200     195     168
       97     103     92     76
     44     53     50     42     34
   18     26     27     23     19     15
 5     13     13     14     9     10     5
```

Page 55 – Break the code

The answer is 871

Page 56 – Wordsearch

```
S E S H A R M O N I C A
A T R O M B O N E T Y G
X P F P B C L Q C R A T
O E L H U L T T E U R K
P M U A I A U O L M U O
H V T R W R B O P K L W
O W E P O I A O O E U S
N R P I A N O E R T L S
E S I Y R E C O R D E R
V I O L A T N W S R L M
H Y T I S T S E O I E R
E O L R Y G U I T A R T
```

Page 57 – Sudoku 4x4

3	1	2	4
2	4	3	1
4	2	1	3
1	3	4	2

Page 58 – Hide and seek

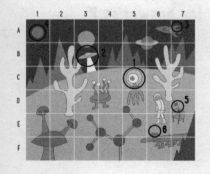

Page 59 – Sudoku 6x6

2	3	5	1	4	6
4	6	1	5	2	3
1	5	2	3	6	4
3	4	6	2	1	5
6	1	3	4	5	2
5	2	4	6	3	1

Page 60 – Spot the difference

Page 61 – Kriss kross

Page 62 – Silhouette

The answer is 3

Page 63 – Monster maths

The answer is 15

Page 64 – Picture reveal

BANANA

Page 65 – Maze

Page 66 – Wordwheel

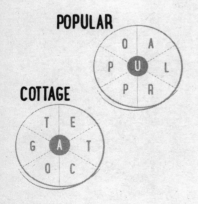

POPULAR

COTTAGE

Page 67 – Number square

8	-	6	x	5	10
÷	■	x	■	x	
4	+	7	x	3	33
x	■	÷	■	÷	
9	+	2	+	1	12
18		21		15	

Page 68 – Sudoku 6x6

4	5	6	1	3	2
3	2	1	4	5	6
1	3	5	2	6	4
6	4	2	3	1	5
2	6	3	5	4	1
5	1	4	6	2	3

Page 69 – Wordsearch

```
W G E T N H P E E L E R
R O A R S B A D G X A T
O K O R S A E W R U T I
L N F D L K U W A U Z M
L I R W E I L C T Z U E
I V Y H E N C X E U G R
N E S I O G S P R P S A
G S N S S T R P R T A A
P F G K H R Z S O E H N
I O P P L A T E S O S O
N R A L X Y U N C E N S
T K N S P A T U L A F W
```

Page 70 – Break the code

WASP

BEETLE

BUTTERFLY

Page 71 – Pile up

Page 72 – Follow the path

The answer is C

Page 73 – Anagram connect

Page 74 – Anagrams

LAUGHTER
FACTORY
KEYBOARD
RECTANGLE
MAGNETISM
QUESTION

Page 75 – Number cross

3		7		9		9		4		4
7	9	2	9	9	2	6	8		1	7	1	5
3		3		5		3		8		0
1	0	3	4		5	9	0	0	4	5	4	9
2		4		0		6			5
8	0	4	2	0	4	3		3	3	2	2	5
	4		2		2		7
4	7	4	8	9		3	0	1	3	8	3	5
0			4		3		8		4
8	4	7	6	5	7	8	4		4	5	4	7
7		1		4		0		6		3
3	9	8	6		4	7	8	5	0	3	2	7
7		7		4		6		2		9

Page 76 – Number square

5	+	8	x	4	52
+		+		+	
9	+	2	-	7	4
x		÷		+	
6	x	1	x	3	18
84		10		14	

Page 77 – Hide and seek

Page 78 – Kakuro example

This page in the book is an example of a kakuro puzzle and how to complete it.

Page 79 – Kakuro

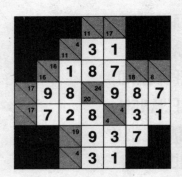

Page 80 – Break the code

To solve this code, you must ignore every second letter, therefore TWHHIQSD becomes THIS, as shown in bold. The message reads:-

THIS CODE USES EXTRA LETTERS TO MAKE IT DIFFICULT TO READ.

Page 81 – Pyramid puzzle

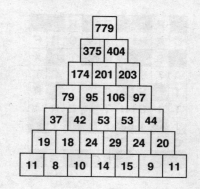

Page 82 – Missing vowels

POPULARITY
VOLUNTEER
BRILLIANT
EYESIGHT
EQUIPMENT
ALLIGATOR

Page 83 – Spot the difference

Page 84 – Crossword

Page 85 – Word ladder

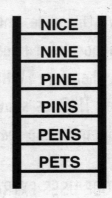

NICE
NINE
PINE
PINS
PENS
PETS

Page 86 – Find the sum

The answer is
29. 30. 43

Page 87 – Shape match

Page 88 - Kriss kross

```
    F   G     M A N D A R I N
G R E E K     U
R   E   R   T U R K I S H
E   N   M   H           S       P
N   C   A   A           I       O
C   H I N D I       S   A       L
H   T       P   S   W   N       I
  J A P A N E S E   E   D U T C H
    L       R   R   D           S
    I       A   S   I       Z   H
    A       B   I   S       E
    N       I   A   H       C
            C   N           H
```

Page 89 - Sudoku 6x6

3	2	4	5	6	1
6	5	1	4	3	2
2	1	3	6	4	5
4	6	5	2	1	3
5	3	6	1	2	4
1	4	2	3	5	6

Page 90 - Break the code

The answer is 368

Page 91 - Anagrams

ENTRANCE
PYRAMID
GREYHOUND
VOLUNTEER
BELIEVE
GRAPEFRUIT

Page 92 – Silhouette

The answer is 5

Page 93 – Kakuro

					4	3
9	10		13	3	1	2
3	2	1	19	6 2	3	1
28 7	9	8	4		13	17
5	16 30	9	7	6	8
14 3	9	2	16	7	9
9 2	7				

Page 94 – Hide and seek

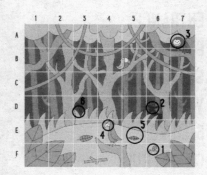

Page 95 – Word splits

PINEAPPLE
THUNDER
DECISION

Page 96 – Number square

6	+	9	+	8	23
÷		x		÷	
3	x	2	+	1	7
x		+		x	
5	x	4	x	7	140
10		22		56	

Page 97 – Picture reveal

SMILEY FACE

Page 98 – Maze

Page 99 – Break the code

WAVE

PEBBLES

LIFEGUARD

Page 100 – Word ladder

MILD
MILL
MALL
MAIL
RAIL
RAIN

Page 101 – Missing vowels

AVALANCHE
AUTOGRAPH
SHEPHERD
WEDNESDAY
INSTANT
PEACEFUL

Page 102 – Number cross

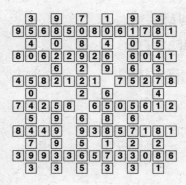

Page 103 – Number square

7	+	3	÷	1	10
+		x		x	
8	÷	4	+	9	11
÷		+		x	
5	x	2	-	6	4
3		14		54	

Page 104 – Sudoku 6x6

2	4	1	6	3	5
3	6	5	1	4	2
6	1	3	2	5	4
4	5	2	3	6	1
1	3	4	5	2	6
5	2	6	4	1	3

Page 105 – Hide and seek

Page 106 – Wordsearch

Page 107 – Crossword

Page 108 – Shape match

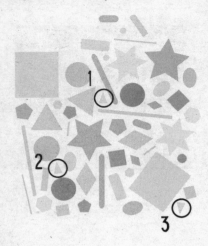

Page 109 – Word splits

AMBULANCE
EMERGENCY
DIFFICULT

Page 110 – Kakuro

Page 111 – Wordwheel

BROTHER

MAJESTIC

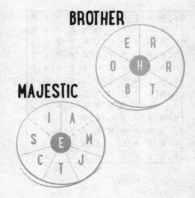

Page 112 – Anagrams

PATIENCE
BATHROOM
PANTHER
PATTERN
GIRAFFE
SHOUDLER

Page 113 – Break the code

The answer is 836

Page 114 – Find the sum

The answer is
35. 38. 39

Page 115 – Word illusion

BODY SOUL

FRESH STALE

ARGUE AGREE

Page 116 – Sudoku 6x6

2	4	5	3	6	1
3	6	1	2	4	5
4	5	2	1	3	6
6	1	3	5	2	4
1	3	4	6	5	2
5	2	6	4	1	3

Page 117 – Kriss kross

Page 118 – Kakuro

Page 119 – Crossword

Page 120 - Break the code

The sentence explains how to solve the puzzle:-

REVERSE EACH PAIR OF LETTERS TO READ THIS.

Page 121 - Anagrams

FIREPLACE

SHADOW

LEARNING

BIRTHDAY

RESTAURANT

EXPERIMENT